D0518046

Skydiving

by Jim Gigliotti

Published by The Child's World®
1980 Lookout Drive
Mankato, MN 56003-1705
800-599-READ
www.childsworld.com

The Child's World®: Mary Berendes, Publishing Director
Shoreline Publishing Group, LLC: James Buckley Jr.,
   Production Director
The Design Lab: Design and production

ISBN: 978-1-60973-211-0
LCCN: 2011928880

Photo credits: Cover: Photos.com.
Interior: AP/Wide World: 23, 24; dreamstime.com:
Dmitrijs Gerciks 7, Zagor 11, Joggie Botma 27; iStock:
4, 12, 16, 28; Photos.com: 8, 15, 20.

Printed in the United States of America
Mankato, Minnesota
July, 2011
PA02094

Table of Contents

Here we go! A skydiver looks back at the plane after jumping.

CHAPTER ONE

On Top of the World!

The small airplane rises off the ground, but that lump in your throat drops to your stomach. Up and up it goes, until the plane reaches five thousand feet. Your palms are sweaty. Ten thousand feet. Your knees are shaking. Thirteen thousand feet. You break out into a cold sweat. The door of the plane opens. The jumper ahead of you goes out. Now it's your turn. You freeze. Your instructor offers a quick word of encouragement. One, two, three . . . jump! And then comes the most **exhilarating** feeling you've ever had. You're almost floating on air! "Woo-hoo!" you scream. You're skydiving!

Does it sound crazy to skydive? Well, yes . . . and no. Statistics show that with proper training and gear, skydiving is not nearly as dangerous as you might think. Skydivers make about three million jumps per year. About 30 people die each year from jumping. That's one death for every 100,000 jumps. And most of those accidents aren't from a parachute failing to open. Rather, they are a result of jumpers not using proper moves, or trying to execute an unsafe **maneuver**.

Modern parachutes have made skydiving very safe.

A skydiver shows the form for enjoying the free fall part of a jump.

So skydiving is pretty safe. It's also a thrilling feeling you can't get from anything else. You might figure it's like being on a roller coaster at your favorite amusement park. You know, a steady uphill climb (the airplane ride) followed by a sudden drop (jumping out of the plane). But skydivers say it's not like that at all. Instead, it's more like walking into a very strong wind . . . only your feet aren't on the ground!

Skydiving began in 1797 in France. André-Jacques Garnerin parachuted out of a hot-air balloon in Paris. The first man to skydive out of an airplane usually is considered to be U.S. Army Captain Albert Berry, in 1912. Today, more than 350,000 people skydive each year. Some of them are one-time jumpers who just want to find out what skydiving feels like. Others are experienced jumpers who own their own chutes and have done hundreds of jumps. Still others are taking an already extreme sport to even more extremes. They go skysurfing and do freestyle skydiving.

Never thought about jumping out of an airplane? Read on to find out what it's like and how you can do it (once you are old enough!).

Military parachutes were shaped like this.

Connected to a trainer, it's thumbs-up
for this tandem jumper.

CHAPTER TWO

Taking the Plunge

Skydiving is an easy sport to get into. You don't need a lot of money or equipment or time to check it out and see if you are interested. Then, if you find that you do like it, you can **invest** in more training and equipment. (You do need to be an adult, however . . . something to look forward to!)

Many first-time skydivers take their first plunge as part of a tandem jump. In a tandem jump, the student and the instructor jump together. The student is connected to the instructor by a **harness**.

The instructor has a parachute big enough for both of them. The instructor worries about when to **deploy**, or release, the parachute. He or she also steers safely to the ground. The student concentrates on getting into the proper position for falling—and on enjoying the ride!

The instruction class for a tandem jump takes less than an hour. Going it alone takes more training. A "static line" jump, for instance, takes about six hours of training. On a static line jump, the skydiver goes alone but is attached to the aircraft by a cable. When the cable runs out, the parachute deploys.

The trainer (in red) will stay near this student for safety.
Then they'll use their own chutes.

From more than two miles in the air, this jump begins with a smile!

In Accelerated Free Fall (AFF) training, skydivers first jump alongside two instructors, but move toward solo flight. The instructors are there to make sure the skydiver opens the parachute properly. Once that's done, they break off to open their own chutes.

How long does a skydive take? That depends on how high you jump from. Here's an example. A skydiver usually jumps from about 13,000 feet.

Hit the Silk!

The first parachutes looked like ice cream cones. The strings holding up the skydiver formed the cone. The parachute billowed above like the top half of a ball. Most parachutes were made of silk. This very strong material is also very lightweight so that the skydiver could carry it easily in a backpack. Military parachutes were made of silk for decades.

That's about 2.5 miles above the ground. A skydiver typically falls at about 120 miles per hour, or 2 miles every minute. The parachute should be deployed about a mile above the ground. The skydiver, then, will free fall—fall without the parachute being open—for less than one minute. Because the parachute slows down the skydiver, the whole ride typically lasts about five minutes. Sometimes, skydivers will go back for several jumps in a single day.

In free fall, skydivers can look at the world spread out below them.

Beginning skydivers don't need to worry about equipment. The cost of going up the first time covers the jump and instruction time. The price also includes the plane ride and equipment rental—including the parachute, of course!

Modern parachutes are made of nylon. They are easy to steer and to land softly. Most are a rectangular "ram-air" design (because air is rammed through individual compartments when the parachute is opened). Steering lines from the parachute let the skydiver turn left or right in the air. This makes it easier to hit the **drop-zone** target!

The skydiver uses the ropes to steer the parachute toward the drop zone.

CHAPTER THREE

Extreme Skydivers

Here's a truly extreme example of skydiving. In 1960, Captain Joseph Kittinger of the United States Air Force skydived from an amazing 102,800 feet. That's more than 19 miles above the ground! It was the highest parachute jump ever made. Captain Kittinger was in free fall for more than four-and-a-half minutes, and the entire jump took about 14 minutes.

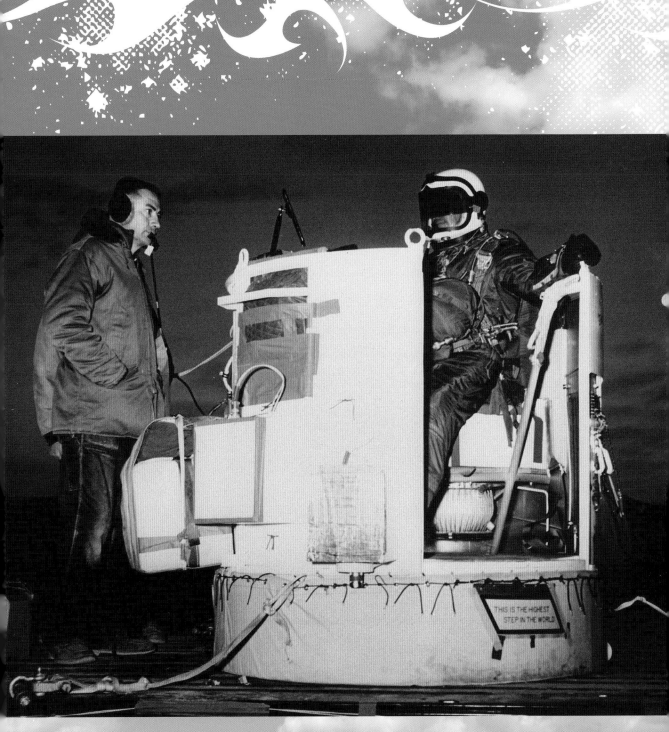

Kittinger jumped from this capsule. The space suit
protected him during his dangerous jump.

Skysurfers jump with cameramen to record their mid-air moves.

Captain Kittinger's jump was very unusual, of course. Some skydivers will jump from as much as 30,000 feet or so. On the other hand, at 120 miles per hour, every 1,000 feet adds another five-and-a-half seconds or so of free fall. Free fall is what experienced skydivers find the most fun. Many of them use that time to perform freestyle stunts in the air. Or they ride a skyboard, much the same way that a snowboarder rides his or her board. They turn and swoop, start and stop, even helicopter—extreme skydivers can perform maneuvers in the air that would make any snowboarder or BMX rider proud!

Today, skydiving generally is done for fun. But there are some skydiving events in which jumpers are judged for their skill and creativity. How can the judges see them way up there? The contestants jump with a cameraman. Teams of jumpers include a skydiver who films the action. He or she is also judged for the quality of the camera work.

Forming up in the air, skydivers create amazing shapes before splitting up.

After gathering up the parachute, it's time to pack it up for another jump!

The United States Parachute Association (USPA) holds the National Skydiving Championships. The event includes Formation Skydiving (with teams of up to 16 jumpers), Freestyle Skydiving, and Accuracy Landing. Other skydivers aim for records. They can gather in groups of dozens in mid-air. They link hands and form complex shapes. Then they all peel off and deploy their chutes.

For most people, though, the appeal of skydiving is not winning a competition. It's overcoming their fear to enjoy the ride of a lifetime.

Skydiving Jobs

Some people skydive for a living. Stunt jumpers work on television and in the movies. In the military, parachute jumpers have been used since the 1940s. (The most famous example was D-Day in World War II. Hundreds of jumpers parachuted into France on the day in 1944 that **Allied** troops began the mission to take back Europe from the Germans.) Smoke jumpers are special kinds of firefighters who parachute into forest fires to help in places trucks and other equipment can't reach.

Glossary

Allied—The collective name of the countries—including Great Britain and Russia—that fought on the United States' side in World War II

deploy—spread out

drop zone—the area where a skydiver aims to land after a jump

exhilarating—excited, thrilling

harness—a safety attachment

invest—to commit time or money for something in return (in this case, the pleasure of skydiving)

maneuver—a movement or tactic

tandem—a group of two acting together

BOOKS

Extreme Skydiving
By Shane Christensen. New York, NY: Crabtree Publishing Company, 2006.
Extreme sports aren't just for the snow or the ground or the water anymore—they've taken to the air now, too, as this book shows.

Skydiving (Action Sports)
By Joanne Mattern. Vero Beach, FL: Rourke Publishing, 2010.
An introduction to skydiving, written for youngsters.

Skydiving (Living on the Edge)
By Shane McFee. New York, NY: PowerKids Press, 2008.
Another look at the sport for young readers.

WEB SITES

For links to learn more about extreme sports: **childsworld.com/links**

Note to Parents, Teachers, and Librarians: We routinely verify our Web links to make sure they are safe and active sites. So encourage your readers to check them out!

Index

About the Author

Jim Gigliotti is a former editor at the National Football League. He has written more than 50 books about sports for youngsters and adults—but he's never had the courage to jump out of an airplane.